Why not Carry on Beading?

Daphne J Ashby
& Jackie Woolsey

June 1999

DEDICATION

This booklet is written for and dedicated to all those who bought our first booklet about beaded amulet purses and promised to buy this one!

Other books by the same authors:

Ribbon Embroidery
      published by David & Charles
      Newton Abbott – September 1996

Creative Embroidery Techniques using Colour through Gold
      published by The Guild of
      Master Craftsman Publications
      Lewes – June 1998

Why not make a Beaded Amulet Purse?
      self-published – June 1998

This booklet first published in the UK in June 1999
by Daphne J Ashby & Jackie Woolsey
The Firs, Dicks Mount, Burgh St Peter, Beccles
NR34 0BU

ISBN 0 947990 97 6

Why not Carry on Beading?

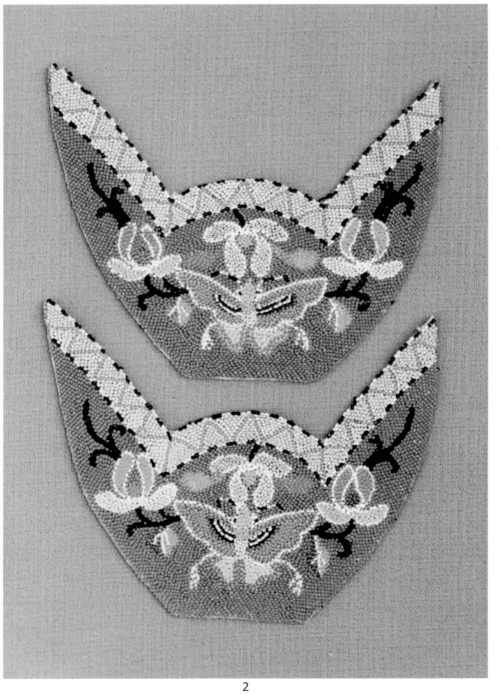

2

INTRODUCTION

In the photograph opposite is a pair of Victorian beaded slipper tops, made when beadwork was very popular in this country. However, much of the inspiration for the type of beading dealt with in this booklet comes from the work of the North American Indians, which is still being produced today.

We were amazed and delighted by the success of the booklet "Why not make a Beaded Amulet Purse?", which we wrote together last year and which seems to have been a jumping off point for many new to this craft, as well as an extension of their beading interests to existing enthusiasts.

In this second booklet, we are responding to many requests for a "follow-up" to include other designs for purses, as well as other beaded pieces to wear, carry or to co-ordinate with each other. Consequently, in addition to a few more purses, this little volume includes designs for matching earrings for two purses, a pen holder worn around the neck, two evening bags, a bracelet and a chatelaine, as well Christmas decorations and other items included simply for inspiration and more ideas for fringes and necklaces.

If this booklet is your <u>first attempt</u> at beading, we would like to suggest that you should start by making the new basic purse design, which is offered at the beginning of this booklet, thus learning the basic "Brick Stitch" and the various fundamental techniques, before trying out the more complicated variations.

Whatever your level of expertise, do carry on beading!

Daphne J Ashby & Jackie Woolsey

June 1999

EQUIPMENT REQUIRED

The main requirement to tackle this craft is time and patience but the end product is so decorative and satisfying that it is certainly worth the effort.

Bugle beads: These are elongated beads and come in a variety of lengths.   The projects illustrated throughout this booklet have been made using bugle beads between 3mm and 9 mm.

Seed beads: There are various suppliers of these particular beads, sometimes called embroidery beads, and there can be a frustrating variation in the sizes of these beads.   When threading the beads, try to pick out those which are as similar as possible and avoid the obviously faulty or oversized.   There is an enormous range of colours, lustres, pearls and bronzed beads and it is an enjoyable task making a choice for the chosen design.

Whilst making the items for this booklet and the previous one, we have noticed considerable variation not only in the sizes of beads contained within one lot but also in the quantities of beads contained in packets, vials and tubes; different manufacturers' packs also vary in weight and this can lead to confusion.   You have been warned!

Throughout the booklet, we have specified "vials" each of which contains approximately 9 grams of beads.

Beading needles: These are available in packets of different sizes and the very finest have eyes which can be very difficult to thread, so a needle threader might also be a good investment.

5

Beading thread: This comes in a variety of thicknesses and it is suggested that the finest gauge and best quality is obtained.   From experience, we would recommend using Beadesign Nymo 'D' which is available in black, white and a number of colours. We have used only black and white for the projects in this booklet: logically, use black for dark beads, including gold, and white for the lighter/pastel shades and silver.

After receiving suggestions and experimenting ourselves, we are not convinced that using beeswax on the beading thread prior to its use is necessary; however, this is a personal choice which is left to you.

Small sharp pointed scissors.

Small tray (a shallow polystyrene dish from the supermarket is ideal) to hold the beads in current use; lining this with felt will make the whole process even easier and help to prevent the beads jumping about.

The clasps used in Chatelaine (page 57) and Bracelet (page 69) were obtained from Ells & Farrer, proprietors of Creative Beadcraft Ltd. 20 Beak Street, London W1R 3HA - medium trigger catches: JF84A 1 and JF84A 2.

One of the projects makes use of empty bead vials - to contain the beading needles and thimble in the Chatelaine - and an empty film cassette container was used as the basic shape for the circular Christmas Tree decoration.   Looking around may give you other inspirational ideas for using beads.

The wooden box in the photograph on page 86 was obtained from The Viking Loom, 22 High Petergate, York YO1 2EH and the leather box from Ambika, 78-79 Troutbeck, Albany Street, London NW1 4EJ.

Most of the seed and bugle beads used in the making of the items shown in this booklet were obtained either from:

> Fabric Flair Ltd
> The Old Brewery
> The Close
> WARMINSTER
> Wiltshire   BA12 9AL

or
> The Bead Merchant
> P.O. Box 5025
> COGGESHALL
> Essex   CO6 1HW

A FEW NOTES BEFORE YOU START

JOINING IN A NEW THREAD

Throughout the working of a piece of beading, you will
need to add new threads.   Do this by weaving the old
thread back through about 10 beads and then start the
new thread by weaving this through a similar number of
beads before joining on a new bead

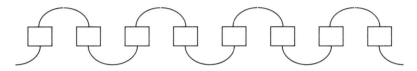

WORKING A SINGLE LAYER, STRAIGHT-EDGED, PIECE OF BEADING

Row 1 will be followed by a second row, the first bead of
which will be slightly in from the edge.

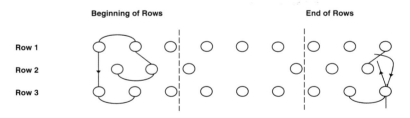

When starting row 3, take the thread up through the
second bead from the end of row 2 and into the bead
next to the end of row 1 and then down through the end
bead.   Then thread two beads on to your needle and
proceed as normal but only going through the second
bead.

At the other end, when you run out of threads between beads, put your needle into the thread which is between the ends of rows 1 and 2.

It is easier if you turn the work in your hand after each row, so you will always be working left to right.

INCREASING THE NUMBER OF BEADS AT A SIDE EDGE

Repeating the above treatment of row 3 on each row would have the effect of increasing the number of beads at the side edge.

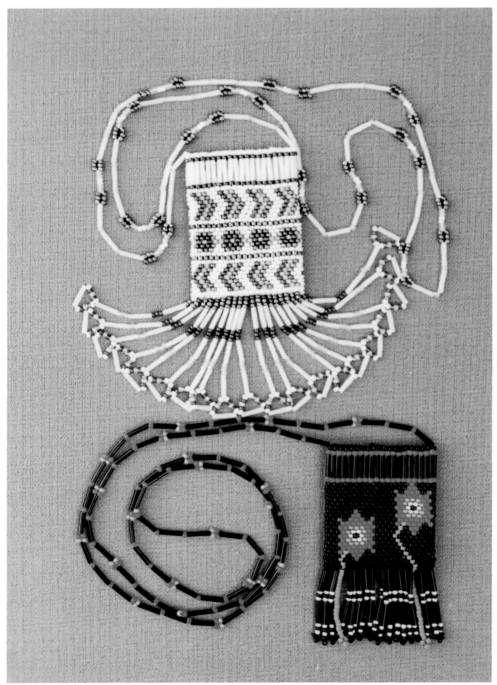

A FIRST BASIC BEADED AMULET PURSE
(if you have not tried beading before, please start here)

For the purse illustrated on the left on the facing page, the instructions for which are given in the sections which follow, you will need:

> 1 vial of white twisted bugle beads
> 2 vials of white seed beads
> 1 vial each of three other colours of seed beads
> (brown, yellow and green)
> 1 reel of white Nymo 'D' beading thread
> 2 beading needles
> Small sharp pointed scissors
> Small tray to hold beads, preferably with felt
> lining

SECTION 1 - THE COLLAR

Cut a generous length of beading thread and, using the beading needle, thread three beads on to the needle in the order: 1 brown seed bead, 1 white twisted bugle bead, 1 brown seed bead and pull the needle through, leaving about six inches of thread hanging.

Hold these beads firmly vertically between the finger and thumb of the left hand.

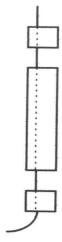

Pick up another set of three beads on the needle, pull the thread through the beads and fold the thread so that the two sets lay side by side between the fingers. Take the needle up through the first set again and down through the second set. (Each bead eventually has three threads passing through it, hence the need for a fine needle and fine thread.)

      * (1) Thread on another set of three beads.
        (2) Take the needle through the previous set
        (3) Then again through the set put on at (1) *

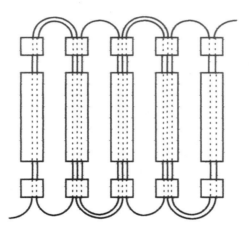

Tension the thread after adding each new set of beads, so that the row created does not flop about. Repeat from * to * until you have 40 sets of beads altogether.

Bend the row round to form a circlet so that you can take the needle back down through the first set of beads and up through set 40. You now have a ring of beads which forms the basic collar and which you can hold over your index and middle fingers ready to start beading the main section.

SECTION 2 - THE MAIN BODY OF THE PURSE

Work a single row of white seed beads on one edge of the collar using the following method:

With the needle and thread which is still attached to the collar:

   **   (1) Thread on a single white seed bead

      (2) Take your needle up behind and over the thread between the next two beads of the previous row.

      (3) Go back down through the white bead and pull the thread firmly. **

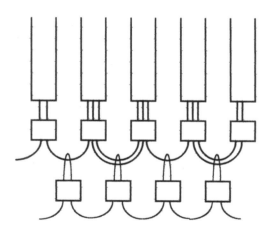

Repeat from ** to ** until you have a complete round of white beads. Take your needle up through the first bead of the round and back down through the last bead of the round again.

Work a single row of white seed beads in the same way around the top of the collar, so now you will have two rows of seed beads above and below the bugle beads, one brown and one white.

Now, using the same method to attach the beads and starting at the top of the chart with Row 1, follow the chart given on page 15, finishing off each round before starting on the next.

When you have finished off your pattern, do not fasten off the thread as you are going to join up the lower edge.

SECTION 3 - CLOSING THE LOWER EDGE

Flatten the body of the purse, centralising your design on one side so that it has a front and a back. Working from one side, go through a bead of the last row, thread a white bead on to the needle, then go through a bead on the other side. Keep doing this, working in alternate directions. This will close the lower edge and give you a row of white beads from which to hang the fringe.

CHART FOR FIRST BASIC PURSE

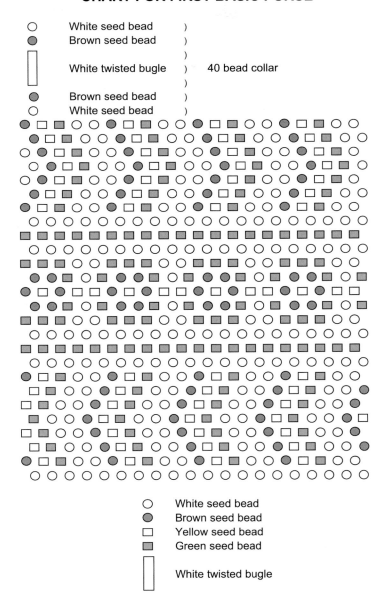

○	White seed bead	)
◉	Brown seed bead	)
		)
▯	White twisted bugle	) 40 bead collar
		)
◉	Brown seed bead	)
○	White seed bead	)

○	White seed bead
◉	Brown seed bead
□	Yellow seed bead
▪	Green seed bead
▯	White twisted bugle

15

SECTION 4 - ADDING THE FRINGE

The fringe can be made of just seed beads, threading different numbers and making the strands different lengths or seed beads + bugle beads or with variations. At this stage, larger beads could also be added.

For the illustrated purse, join a thread so that it emerges at one end of the lower edge and pass the needle through the end joining white bead.   Thread all the beads required for the first strand of the fringe on to the needle, in accordance with the diagram shown below (see main chart for key to bead colours), pulling the needle back through the first twelve beads again after adding the middle section of 11 beads.   Pass the needle through the joining white bead on the purse again from the opposite direction.   Repeat this 19 more times to give a 20-strand fringe.

SECTION 5 - THE NECKLACE

For this, you need two beading needles with long threads. Join the two at the top corner of the purse and thread both needles through the first five beads:

1 white twisted bugle,
1 yellow seed
1 white twisted bugle
1 yellow seed,
1 white twisted bugle

Then thread 3 green seed beads on to each needle and then pass the first needle back through the 3 green seed beads on the second needle and then through the first set again - see the diagram below.

Now, pass both needles through 2 gold seed beads, 2 white seed beads and two gold seed beads and repeat from * to * again.   Repeat the entire sequence again as many times as necessary to give the required length of necklace and then fasten off, joining the threads on to the opposite edge of the purse.

Alternative designs for necklaces are given throughout this booklet (and in "Why not make a Beaded Amulet Purse?) but you could also make up your own.

ENJOY WEARING YOUR BEADED AMULET PURSE!

<u>CARRIE'S PURSE</u>   (with grateful thanks to Carrie Evans for designing and making this purse)

The design for this striking beaded amulet purse (pictured on the right in the photograph on page 10) incorporates four poppies, the stalks of which extend down into the fringe, against a background of sophisticated black.

<u>Materials</u>
1 vial of black bugle beads
1 vial of black seed beads
1 vial of red seed beads
1 vial of green seed beads
86 orange seed beads
24 metallic gold seed beads

1 reel of beading thread Nymo D in black

<u>Equipment:</u>
2 beading needles
Small sharp pointed scissors
Small tray to hold beads, preferably with felt lining

THE COLLAR

Referring to the instructions for the First Basic Purse, use the following beads to make a 40 bead collar:

              1 red seed bead
              1 black bugle bead
              1 red seed bead

Chart for Carrie's Purse

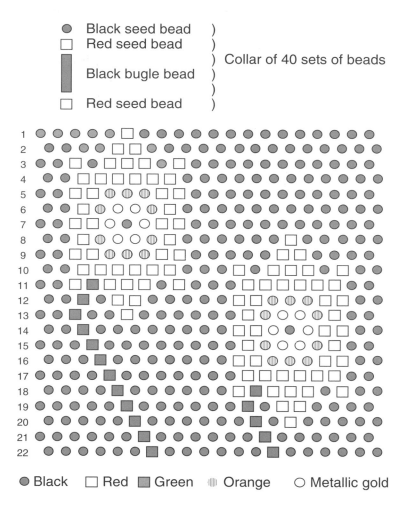

● Black seed bead)
□ Red seed bead)
▮ Black bugle bead) Collar of 40 sets of beads
□ Red seed bead)

● Black   □ Red   ▮ Green   ⦀ Orange   ○ Metallic gold

THE MAIN BODY OF THE PURSE

Work a single row of black seed beads along the top edge of the collar.

Starting with Row 1, follow the chart on page 19, finishing off each round before starting on the next.

JOINING THE LOWER EDGE OF THE PURSE

Flatten the body of the purse, ensuring that the flowers in the design are centrally placed.
Working from one side, go through a bead of the last row, thread a black seed bead on to the needle, then go through a bead on the other side.   Keep doing this, working in alternate directions.   This will close the lower edge and give you a row of black seed beads from which to hang the fringe.   (See the instructions for joining the lower edge of the purse – page 14.)

THE FRINGE

Join a thread so that it emerges at one end of the lower edge and pass the needle through the end joining bead. Thread all the beads required for the first strand of the fringe onto the needle and pull the thread through; then, missing the last three seed beads, pass the needle and thread back through the rest of the beads again and through the joining bead on the purse from the opposite direction.   Repeat for each strand, positioning the two all green seed bead strands directly beneath the stalk of the poppies in the purse.

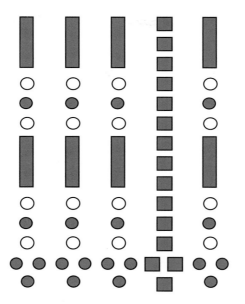

![Black bugle bead] Black bugle bead

● Black seed bead
○ Metallic gold seed bead
■ Green seed bead

NECKLACE

When the fringe is complete, you are ready to make the necklace and, for this, you need two beading needles with long threads (1.5-2m).   Join both at one top corner of the purse weaving the threads through the beads as before.

(Refer to the instructions given for the necklace in the basic purse on page 16.)

*On to one needle, thread:

    1 black bugle
    1 red seed bead
    1 black bugle
    1 red seed bead
    1 black bugle

With the second needle, go through the first five beads and then thread

    1 orange seed bead
    1 red seed bead

on to each needle.   With the second needle, go back down through the two beads threaded on with the first needle and up through the two threaded on with the second.*   Repeat the whole process from * to * until the necklace is the required length.

(An alternative method of making the necklace is to thread all the beads for the entire length required on to one needle and then, with the second needle and thread, to follow the procedure outlined above.)

BEADED AMULET PURSE WITH FLAP AND MATCHING EARRINGS

This purse has a flap fastening and the luxury of matching earrings (shown in the photograph overleaf), creating a set which will surely draw admiring glances!

Materials (for necklace and earrings)
1 vial 9 mm brown bugle beads
1 vial green seed beads
1 vial yellow glass seed beads
1 vial mottled brown seed beads
1 vial larger green 3-sided beads

1 reel Nymo D beading thread in black

Equipment
2 beading needles
Pair of earring fitments
Small sharp embroidery scissors
Tray for beads, preferably with felt lining

BEADING

Work a basic collar of 40 sets of 1 yellow seed bead, 1 brown bugle bead and 1 yellow seed bead as described previously (see page 11) with a row of green seed beads above and below.

Work rows 1 to 18 inclusive of the body of the purse from the chart given on page 25.

Design chart for purse with flap and matching earrings

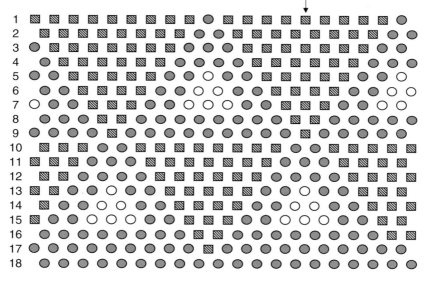

- ◉ Green seed bead)
- ○ Yellow seed bead)
- ▨ Brown bugle bead) 40 bead collar
- ○ Yellow seed bead)
- ◉ Green seed bead)

Centre point

▨ Brown bugle bead

- ◉ Green seed bead
- ○ Yellow seed bead
- ▨ Brown seed bead

Row 19: pick up a yellow seed bead, a brown bugle bead and a yellow seed bead on the needle and, using sets of the same beads, work as for the collar but joining onto the purse through the last row of seed beads.   Add a row of green seed beads.

JOINING THE LOWER EDGE

Position the pattern centrally and join the bottom of the purse with another row of green seed beads – see page 14 of basic purse for instructions.

FRINGE

Using seed beads and larger beads:

Row 1:   Pass needle through the first joining bead and pick up the following beads:

brown / yellow / green / yellow / brown / yellow / large bead / brown / yellow / green / yellow / brown / yellow / green / yellow / brown / yellow / green / yellow / brown / large bead / green / yellow / brown / yellow / green / yellow /

Now pick up five brown seed beads and take needle back up through all the other fringe beads and back through the joining bead.

Row 2:   Pass needle through the following beads:

* brown / yellow / green / yellow / brown / yellow / green / yellow / brown / yellow / green / yellow / brown / large bead * repeat from * to *

Now pick up five brown seed beads and take needle back up through all the other fringe beads and back through the joining bead as for Row 1.

Repeat these two fringe rows until each of the joining beads has been used. (20 rows in all.)

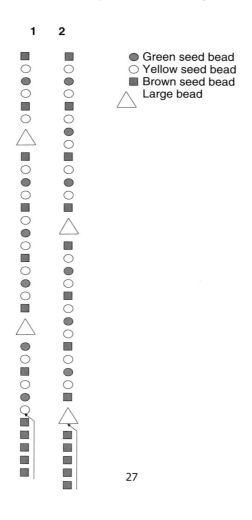

● Green seed bead
○ Yellow seed bead
■ Brown seed bead
△ Large bead

FLAP

Join in a beading thread to come out at one side edge of the purse and work along the back of the purse, following the chart for this design below.

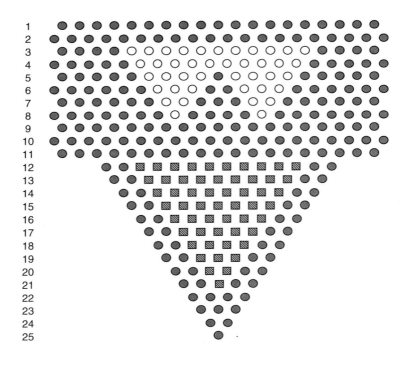

● Green seed bead
○ Yellow seed bead
▨ Brown seed bead

Add a loop of ten green seed beads and fasten off the thread securely.

Fold flap to the front and mark the position of the loop, joining in a thread at this point on the front of the purse.

Pick up: two brown seed beads / one larger bead / five brown / one larger bead and one brown bead.

Missing the brown bead, go back through the other beads and work a second set in the same way, fastening off the thread securely.

Fasten the flap by putting one line of beads on the purse through the loop on the flap.

NECKLACE

Join two beading needles with long threads to the top corner of the purse, pick up one yellow, one brown and one seed bead on both needles and then follow the chart below:

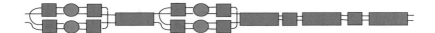

EARRINGS

Leaving an end of beading thread of about 8", work as for the collar of the purse (see page 23) until eight sets of beads are in place.
Work a row of green seed beads along one edge and then work a triangle, following the chart:

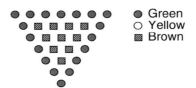

● Green
○ Yellow
▨ Brown

Run the thread through the beads on one side of the triangle and back down through a set of beads on the collar.   Work a row of green seed beads - there will be seven beads in this row.

FRINGE

Using the row of seven green seed beads, work a fringe as shown below:

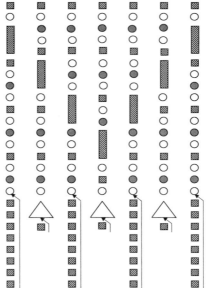

Using the starting end of the thread, sew the beaded earrings on to the fitment.

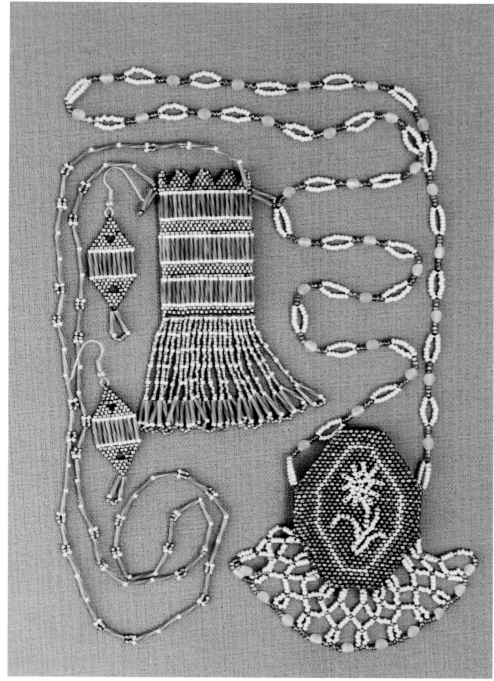

31

BEADED AMULET PURSE AND EARRINGS
with delica beads

The introduction of twisted bugle beads into the body of the purse and the use of delica beads, gives this design a distinctly different "look" and, with the added attraction of matching earrings, will make this combination a pleasure to wear.   (Photograph on left on previous page.)

Materials (for necklace and earrings)
1 vial twisted bugle beads in Mauve
1 vial each of delica beads in: white
                                        gold metallic
                                        mauve

1 reel white Nymo D beading thread
Pair of earring fitments

Equipment
2 beading needles
Embroidery scissors
Tray to hold beads, lined with felt

BEADING

Make the collar of the purse using 1 white delica bead, 1 twisted bugle and 1 white delica bead, in the usual way (see page 11) until you have 40 sets of beads.   Take the thread back up through the first set of beads and back through the 40th set of beads .

Work a row of gold metallic delica beads along the top edge of the collar then, above this row, at the top of the purse, work a row of triangles outlined with gold metallic delica beads with mauve delicas inside, as follows:

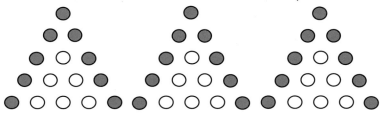

● gold metallic delica   ○ mauve delica

Go back to the lower edge of the collar and add four rows of delica beads in the following order:

> 1 row gold metallic
> 2 rows mauve
> 1 row gold metallic

Thread on three beads - 1 white delica, 1 twisted bugle and 1 white delica - followed by a second group of the same beads. Go up through the metallic bead in the row above and down the one to its left and through the first group of three and back up through the second group of three.

In other words, this is worked as for the collar but going up and down through the beads in the previous row, as shown in the following diagram:

33

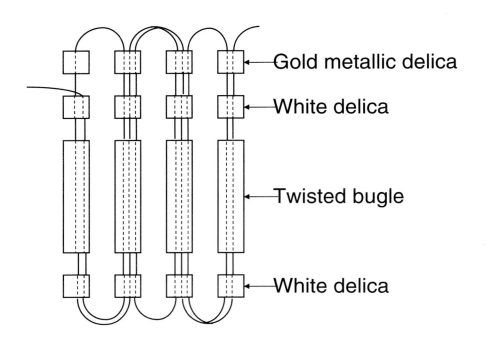

Gold metallic delica

White delica

Twisted bugle

White delica

Carry on like this until you have gone all the way round the purse. Repeat the four rows of delica beads as before and then the whole sequence again - see photograph.

Work a row of gold metallic delicas followed by a row of mauve delicas and then join the lower edge of the purse with mauve delicas (see page 14 for instructions on joining the lower edge.)

FRINGE

Work the fringe following the chart at the top of the next page; there is a group of twisted bugle and delica beads at the end of each strand of the fringe - this is added by passing the needle through the group in sequence and then back up through the fringe strand.

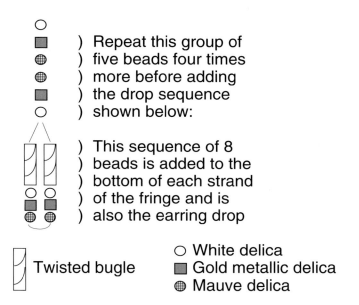

) Repeat this group of
) five beads four times
) more before adding
) the drop sequence
) shown below:

) This sequence of 8
) beads is added to the
) bottom of each strand
) of the fringe and is
) also the earring drop

Twisted bugle

○ White delica
■ Gold metallic delica
⊕ Mauve delica

HANGINGS

Join the necklace thread on and work the small hangings using a gold metallic delica bead, a twisted bugle, one gold metallic delica, one mauve and one gold metallic delica bead, followed by a second twisted bugle.   Take the thread up through the top row of beads, ready to start the necklace.   (A second hanging is worked when the end of the necklace is joined to the purse.)

NECKLACE
Using two needles and two long lengths of beading thread and following the diagram given overleaf (*) on to one needle, thread:

1 twisted bugle
1 white delica
1 twisted bugle
1 white delica
1 twisted bugle

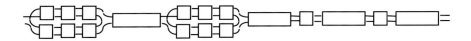

Pass the second needle through the same beads and then (**) thread:

1 white delica
1 gold metallic delica
1 mauve delica

on to each needle. With the second needle, go down through the three delicas threaded on to the first needle and then back up through the three threaded on to the second needle.(**)

Thread both needles through a twisted bugle bead and then repeat from (**) to (**) (*).

Repeat the whole sequence from (*) to (*) until the necklace is the required length. Add a hanger to match the first one at the point where the end of the necklace is joined to the purse.

EARRINGS

Using the same set of three beads as for the collar of the purse, work until you have ten sets of beads.

Add a row of gold metallic delicas above the collar (9 delicas) and go on to work the three joined upright triangles as shown below:

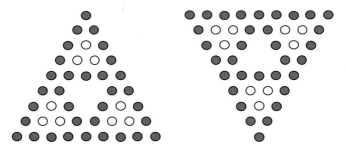

For top of earring   For bottom of earring

Invert the earring and repeat the above procedure until you have only a single bead. Add the sequence of beads as given for the bead drop at the end of each strand of the fringe:

Make a second earring in the same way.

OCTAGONAL PURSE

This purse (photograph on page 31) experiments with an entirely new shape and has a different fringe with a lacey, net-like effect.   The flower decoration is made of superimposed beadwork and the fringe and necklace incorporate decorative beads.

Materials
Seed beads   2 vials lustre blue
Seed beads   1 vial silver
Decorative beads   1 vial

1 reel Nymo D beading thread in black

Equipment
2 beading needles
Small sharp embroidery scissors
Tray for holding beads, lined with felt

BEADING

Work the first 15 rows of the body part of the purse from the chart given on page 39; put to one side and work a second piece in the same way.

16th row: work this across the first part of the purse and straight on across the second part, joining the two together into a circle at the end of the row.

Rows 17 to 26 inclusive are worked in this way going right round the purse.   From row 27 you will again be working in two sections.   Row 27 will have 23 beads, row 28 will have 22 beads and row 29 will

Octagonal Purse with flower emblem

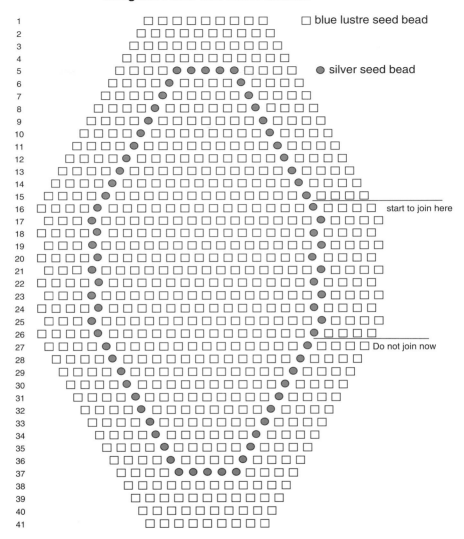

□ blue lustre seed bead

● silver seed bead

start to join here

Do not join now

39

only have 21 beads.   Continue to decrease in this way until row 41 when you will have only 9 beads.

When you have completed one side move on to the other set of beads and work side two. Before you join the lower edges of the purse work the superimposed decoration.

SUPERIMPOSED DECORATION

Join on a new thread and come up to the front of the purse about 8 rows down from the row of five silver beads and, using silver seed beads, work a group of ten beads for the flower centre. Then radiate out using 3 beads each time to make the flower petals. Ten in all. Add a stem of 8 beads and then three more lines of beads to suggest the foliage:

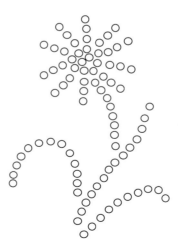

Join the purse down the sloped side, along the base and up the other side, adding "joining" beads as in the original design. (see page 14).

FRINGE

Start at one side of the purse , going through the first joining bead, add * 4 silver, 1 blue, 4 silver , 1 blue (this is the bead that will be used to join to the next drop of the fringe), 4 silver, 1 blue, 4 silver, 3 blue, 1 decorative bead , 3 blue, 4 silver , 1 blue , 4 silver; go into the blue bead at the centre of the first drop (marked in diagram) to make a loop , then add 4 silver, 1 blue, 4 silver*.

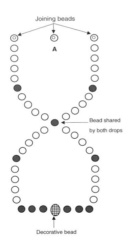

Miss one joining bead and go into the next and repeat from * to *.   After the first group as illustrated, miss two joining beads at point A until ten groups have been worked then miss only one joining bead and work group as before.

NECKLACE

Join the two needles and threads at the point where the increasing has finished and the purse is joined and worked in the round.

Start by threading 8 silver beads onto each thread, then both threads go through the 3 blue beads, the decorative bead and the other 3 blue beads before another 8 silver beads are added onto each thread. The second thread will then go back through the group of 8 beads on the first needle and through the second group again to lock it - thus avoiding the loss of a lot of beads should the necklace break.

Repeat until the necklace is the required length.

BEADED PENHOLDER

Now, at last, the perfect solution to knowing exactly where your pen is all the time and it will be extremely difficult for anyone to borrow it without you knowing! A really attractive spiraling pattern on the holder, an unusual necklace and a beaded ball topping its fringe, all contribute to make this penholder a most attractive and useful item.   (Photograph on previous page.)

Materials
2 vials 9 mm bugle beads in dark grey
1 vial 6 mm bugle beads in silver
1 vial each of seed beads in: medium grey
                                   mottled red
                                   silver
                                   yellow gold

1 reel Nymo D beading thread in black
Wooden bead (about the size of a large pea)
Seed bead vial (we used a Bead Merchant 10gm vial)

Equipment
2 beading needles
Small sharp pointed scissors
Tray to hold beads, preferably with felt lining

BEADING

Work the collar as shown for the basic beaded amulet purse, (page 11) using a silver seed bead, a dark grey bugle bead and a silver seed bead.

It took 25 groups to go around the illustrated pen holder.

Work a single row of grey seed beads above and below the collar.

For the body part of the holder, work in groups of five seed beads, as shown on the following chart, with each row moving back one bead to form the spiral pattern. Work 35 rows in this way and then check that, when the top collar is repeated, it will be sufficient to cover the vial.

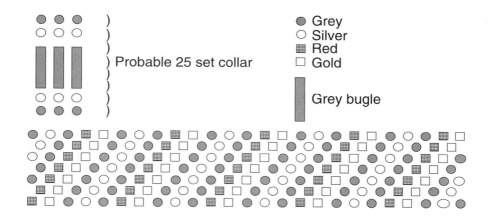

To form the base of the holder, work a triangle of beads on the first five beads round the base. Repeat this with the next 5 beads and so on, until five triangles have been formed.

Join the triangles together, going through each of the single seed beads at the point of each triangle.

TOP COLLAR DECORATION

Form the collar decoration by working into the row of grey seed beads at the base of the collar.   Join in the thread, in the usual way, and then thread onto the needle:

    1 grey seed bead
    1 silver bugle bead
    1 grey seed bead
    1 silver seed bead.

Missing the last bead added, pass the needle back through the other beads and the medium grey bead of the collar.   Bring the needle down through the next collar bead and repeat until you have been right round.

COVERING THE WOODEN BEAD

Take the wooden bead and a long double thread, knotted at the end.   Go up through the bead with the needle and then through the knotted end.   Edge the knot up inside the bead.

Thread on as many beads as is necessary to reach from the hole at one end of the bead to the hole at the other end.   Run the needle through the centre of the wooden bead and keep repeating this process until the wooden bead is entirely covered.

Ensure that none of the seed beads slips into the hole in the wooden bead.

For the pen holder shown in the photograph, rows of

> grey
> silver
> grey
> red
> and yellow gold

 seed beads were used.

Sew the bead firmly to the base of the holder below the triangles.

TASSEL FRINGE

Using the lowest bead of each of the strands used to cover the wooden bead, work the tassel fringe.   After going through the seed bead on the wooden bead, put the following on the needle:

> 5 seed beads – grey, silver, grey, red, gold
> a dark grey bugle bead
> 5 seed beads - grey, silver, grey, red, gold
> a dark grey bugle bead
> 5 seed beads - grey, silver, grey, red, gold
> a dark grey bugle bead
> 3 seed beads – red, gold, red
> a dark grey bugle bead

Take the needle up through the fringe starting at the third group of five seed beads - marked with * on the diagram.

Go back up through the seed bead at the start of the fringe and down through the next seed bead.   Carry on in this way until you have a fringe hanging from each of the lower seed beads on the ball of the tassel.

NECKLACE

Join a long thread up on the top edge of the holder ready to start making the necklace.   Thread onto the needle:

> a silver seed bead
> a dark grey bugle bead
> a silver seed bead

and go down into the top row of the collar and back through the three beads and (working as for the original collar) continue until you have five repeats.

Next, take seed beads in the following colours:

> grey
> silver
> grey
> red

        yellow gold
        red
        grey
        silver
        grey

Then take
        a silver seed bead
        a dark grey bugle bead
        and a silver seed bead

followed by the above sequence of nine seed beads again
and thread the needle through the fifth repeat of the last
block.

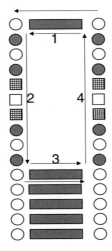

Repeat this sequence until the necklace is the required
length.   Fasten off the thread in the top row of seed
beads in the main part of the holder.

50

BEADED CHRISTMAS TREE DECORATIONS

Use red, gold and black beads to create these spectacular tree decorations to bring a wonderful sparkle to your Christmas festivities and prove a spectacular talking point for all who see them.

Study the photograph of the three matching decorations on the facing page for inspiration and information as to the main details of the construction; the instructions which follow are for the <u>circular decoration</u>.

<u>Materials</u>
1 vial 9 mm bugle beads in black
1 vial 9 mm twisted bugle beads in metallic gold
1 vial each of 3 mm bugle beads in: metallic gold
                                            black
1 vial each of seed beads in: black
                                      red
                                      metallic gold

1 reel Nymo D beading thread in black

<u>For making up the decoration</u>
Empty 35 mm film container
Small pieces of 2 mm card
Small piece of thin wadding

<u>Equipment</u>
2 beading needles
Small sharp pointed scissors
Tray to hold beads, preferably with felt lining

BEADING

Work the collar as shown for the basic beaded amulet purse (page 11) using red, black and gold seed beads, as well as the 9mm and 3 mm bugle beads listed: follow the chart shown below and repeat this section four times before joining the ends to form the collar.

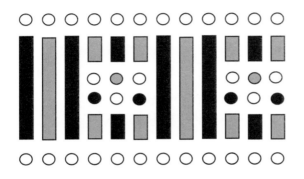

Key: ○ Gold seed bead   ▮ Black bugle bead
        ● Black seed bead
        ○ Red seed bead   ▯ Gold bugle bead

Work two rows of gold seed beads above and below the collar - see page 13 for instructions on how to add these beads to the collar.

The triangular pattern which forms the main body of each decoration is formed by using the following 11-row chart:

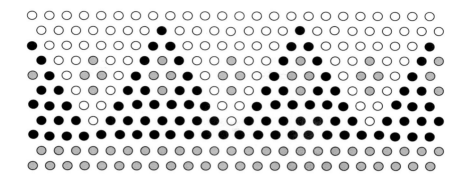

Work a further two rows of gold seed beads. Now repeat the collar, joining it on to the last row of gold seed beads.

Return to the top of the hanging and work a row of red seed beads. Then work from chart below, over the first 16 beads, making a first triangle. Then work two more triangles, each over 16 seed beads.

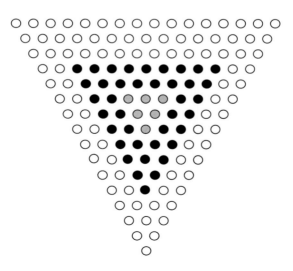

With a thread coming down through a gold seed bead at the lower edge, thread on the beads as shown in the diagram below.

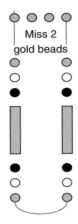

Keep working round the lower edge of the decoration, going into a seed bead and missing two each time. From below, these lines of beads will look like the spokes of a wheel:

When all the spokes have been worked (16) and going around the ring of gold beads at the lower edge, make a 'fringe' by hanging the sequence of beads shown below from each gold bead.

Finishing the decoration

Cut a circle of card the size of the container top. Cut a circle of thin wadding the same size, one slightly smaller and one slightly smaller again. Pile the three shapes on the card, smallest first, then the medium followed by the largest circle. Cover the padded circle with gold fabric, gather it round on the underside. Gently push the container down inside the decoration with the gold padded surface at the top.

Join the beaded triangles together (enclosing the container) by going through the single red seed at the top of each triangle, adding two red seed beads between each, making a circle of 9 beads.

Now join on a gold seed bead, a 3 mm black bugle bead and a gold seed bead and work as for the collar of the first amulet in this booklet - page 11 - until 30 groups of beads have been added. Make this collar into a loop for hanging the decoration by working into the first group of three beads and then fasten off.

The other two decorations with the same pattern were worked in a similar way but one over a made up square cardboard shape and the other using a triangular shape. The fourth decoration with blue and gold beads, which was worked by Claire Dawkins (to whom we offer our grateful thanks) is just to give you another idea using a different colour combination.

BEADED CHATELAINE

This is really something special.   A wonderful collection of beaded containers for needles, thread bobbins, scissors and a thimble, all suspended on a series of beaded hangers from a bead-decorated band to wear on a belt.   Perhaps the ultimate gift for a beading friend?

Materials

5 vials of navy blue seed beads
2 vials of gold seed beads
2 vials of turquoise seed beads
2 vials of copper seed beads

2 reels of Nymo D beading thread in black
5 trigger clasps (medium-size)

Equipment

2 Beading needles
Sharp scissors
Navy blue satin ribbon to make belt hanger
Small piece extra heavy interfacing

MAKING THE HANGING FRAMEWORK

Work seven rectangles according to the following chart:

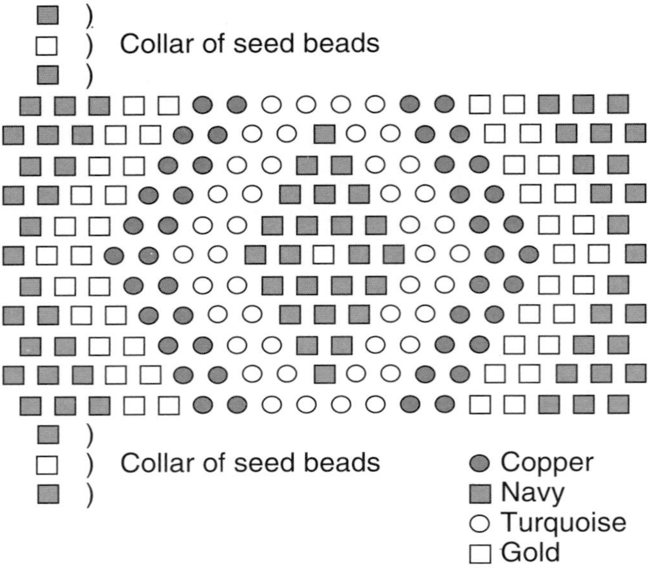

■)
□) Collar of seed beads
■)

● Copper
■ Navy
○ Turquoise
□ Gold

■)
□) Collar of seed beads
■)

Work another four rectangles using the next chart:

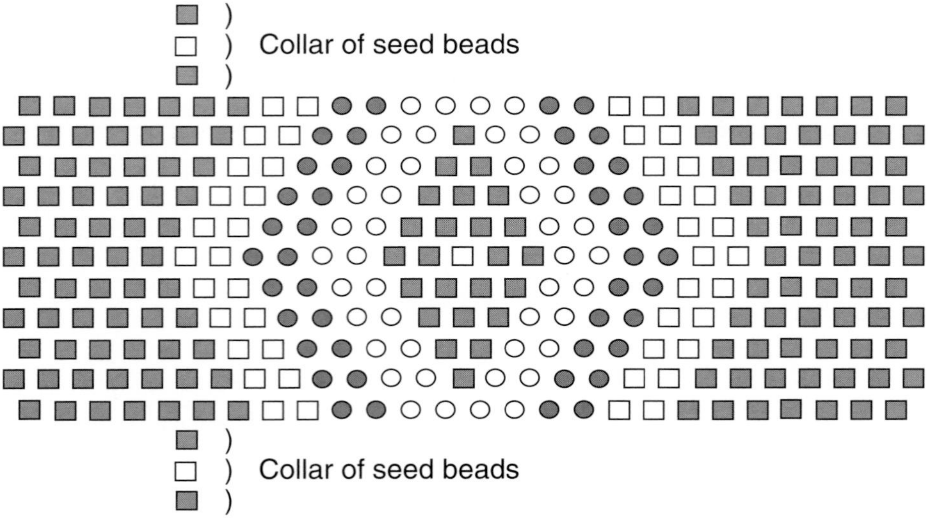

■)
□) Collar of seed beads
■)

■)
□) Collar of seed beads
■)

58

The diagram given below shows the position of the seven smaller rectangles – A, B, C, D, E, F and G – and the three slightly larger rectangles – H, I and J

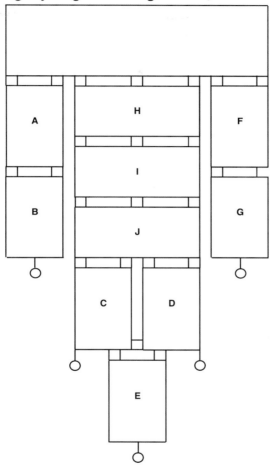

Now work the largest rectangle, which will be made up into the main hanging section to be worn on a belt. Start with a collar made up of 58 sets of three seed beads: one navy one gold and one navy. Then add the body of the section following the chart given overleaf:

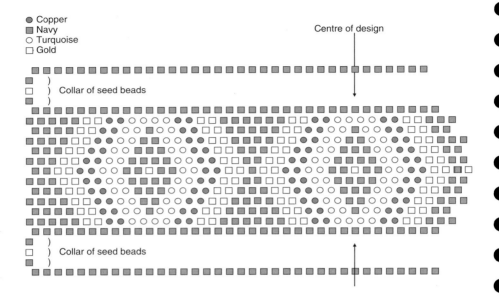

Copper
Navy
Turquoise
Gold

Centre of design

Collar of seed beads

Collar of seed beads

MAKING UP THE CHATELAINE

Each section is joined to the next with two sets of beads: 1 navy seed, 1 gold seed and 1 navy seed, on each end.

Once all the sections of the chatelaine are made, join each to the next by the additional sets of beads on the ends of the top edges. Refer to the diagram showing all the sections.

Cut a small piece of extra heavy interfacing to the size of the main hanging section and cover it on one side with the ribbon, turning the edges over. Lay the beaded section over the non-covered side and attach going into the beads on the edge and the covered interfacing. Cut two lengths of the ribbon and turning the edges in, join together to make a double-layer the size of the front.

Then stitch this to the front section just along the top and lower edges. This will give a channel through which a narrow belt can be threaded.

The five containers are suspended from clasps hung on the rectangles of the chatelaine using handles of navy, copper and gold seed beads, with loops of 10 copper seed beads at the middle of the three copper seed beads in the centre.   The four shorter handles are formed by following the diagram below:

Thread on:

Repeat this sequence twice more and then add:

With a second needle, thread on:

and go back down the similar sequence on the first handle thread and back up through the ones just added – this is to "lock" the section.

Continue doing this until you reach the centre set of copper beads – go through two of them and then add on 10 more copper beads to make a hanging loop and go back through the centre bead and the third bead and proceed as before, until you reach the end of the handle. Attach the clasps in the position as shown on the finished chatelaine.

Scissors Case

Work a collar of one navy, two gold and one navy seed beads until you have 38 sets of beads. Join the collar and add a single row of navy seed beads around the top and lower edges.

Working only on half (19) of the beads, which will be either the front or back of the scissors case, add beads in accordance with the following chart, decreasing one bead on each row for 14 rows. Then repeat rows 13 and 14 until you have 21 rows of navy seed beads (9 repeats).

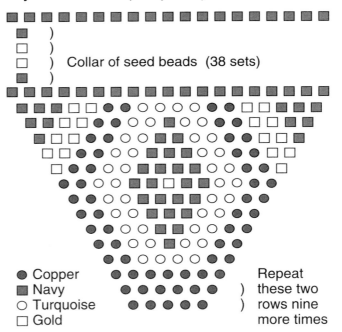

- ● Copper
- ■ Navy
- ○ Turquoise
- □ Gold

Repeat
) these two
) rows nine
more times

Repeat this on the other set of 19 beads.

Join up the two sides and along the lower edge; the handle is worked as shown on page 61 but two extra repeats are needed to make it longer.

Bobbin Cases

By following the chart shown below and working the shape twice for each, make two bobbin cases for the chatelaine.

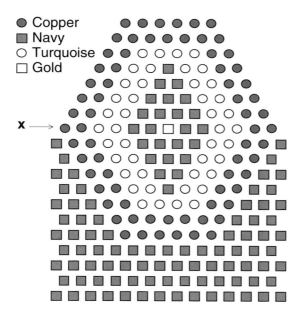

Gusset

Work a gusset over four beads, starting with a collar of three seed beads: one navy, one gold and one navy.

Collar for gusset: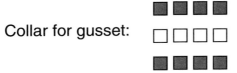

Then proceed with navy beads until the gusset is the required length to go right round. Remember that every other row will only have three seed beads. Repeat the collar at the other end.

This navy gusset is then sewn between the two bobbin case shapes, starting where the navy beads appear on the sides – marked X on the chart.

Above each seed bead collar on the gusset, work a triangle of navy seed beads, starting with a row of three and then decreasing by one on each row (3 – 2 – 1):

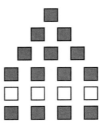

Now work a handle for each of the bobbin cases, continuing on from the single seed bead on the triangle, as shown on page 61.

Fasten both threads on to the single bead of the triangle at the other side of the bobbin case.

Needle Case

This bead needle case is worked around a 10 gram bead vial cut down to 6.5 cm long.

Start by making a collar of 24 sets of one navy, two gold, one navy, two gold and one navy seed beads. Join the collar and add a single row of navy seed beads around the top and lower edges.

Follow the chart below, then repeat rows 2-11 twice before adding one row of navy seed beads, two rows of gold and another of navy.

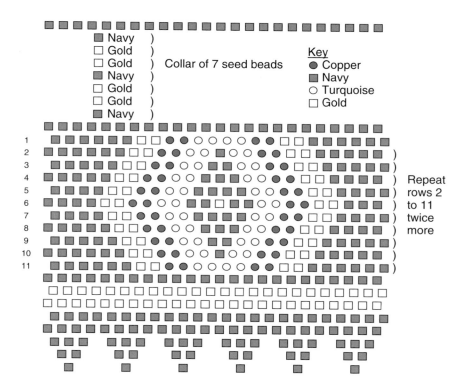

■ Navy)
□ Gold)
□ Gold) Collar of 7 seed beads
■ Navy)
□ Gold)
□ Gold)
■ Navy)

Key
● Copper
■ Navy
○ Turquoise
□ Gold

Repeat rows 2 to 11 twice more

Work the six triangles around the lower edge as shown. Join the single beads together, forming the base of the case for the needle container. Work a handle as shown on page 61.

Thimble Case

The thimble case is worked around a 2 cm diameter bead vial cut down to 3 cm long.

Start by making a collar of 32 sets of one navy, two gold and one navy seed beads. Join the collar and add a single row of navy seed beads around the top and lower edges.

Follow the chart given on page 67.

Join the four single beads at the bottom of the triangles to form the base of the thimble case.

Insert the bead vial to contain the thimble.

Work a handle as shown on page 64.

Thimble Case

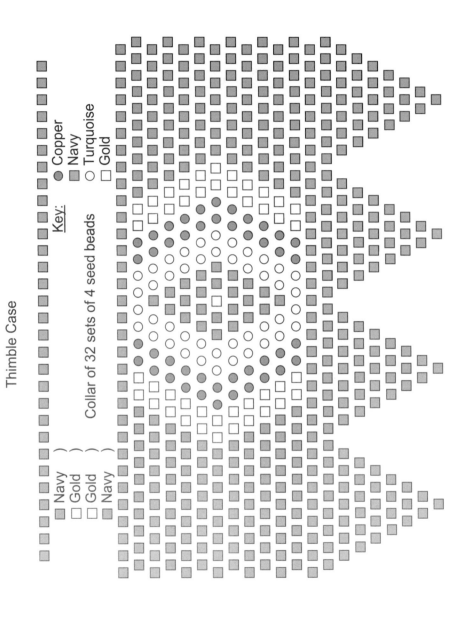

Key:
● Copper
■ Navy
○ Turquoise
□ Gold

Collar of 32 sets of 4 seed beads

■ Navy)
□ Gold)
□ Gold)
■ Navy)

BRACELET

This elegant bracelet will surely become a firm favourite – make several up in colours to co-ordinate with all your outfits?

Materials

1 vial each of: Gold seed beads
                   Green seed beads
                   Brown seed beads
                   Copper seed beads
                   Yellow seed beads

1 reel of Nymo D beading thread in black
1 trigger clasp (medium-size)

Equipment

Beading needle and sharp scissors

Beading

Work a straight collar of five seed beads (one green, one gold, one copper, one gold and one green) until there are 84 sets; at this stage, check that the collar goes around your wrist and add extra green beads at each end if necessary.

Work a single row of green seed beads above and below the collar. The first row of the pattern added below the row of green seed beads will contain 84 beads, the next 83 beads, the next 84 and so on, as shown alongside.

Make the bracelet by following the chart given on page 71.

Note that two green beads are added at the beginning and end of row 1 and every other row, whereas row 2 and all the even numbered rows have two green seed beads at the beginning but only one at the end. Look carefully at the photograph for the number of pattern repeats.

When the pattern rows have been completed, add a row of green seed beads and then repeat the five seed bead collar, going back up into the last row.

Make a loop of 15 copper beads in the middle of one edge of the bracelet and fix a trigger clasp in the middle of the opposite edge.

B R A C E L E T

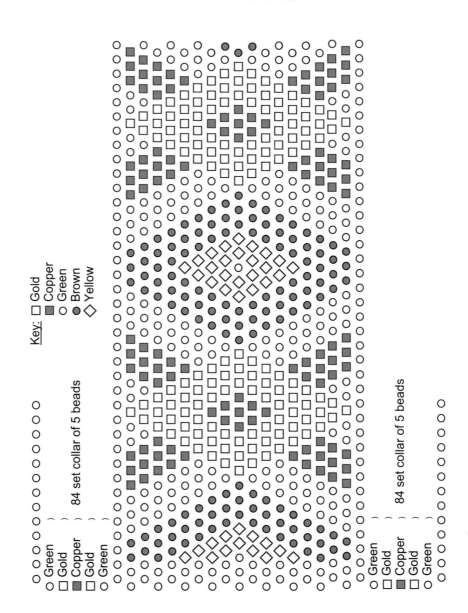

Key: □ Gold
     ■ Copper
     ○ Green
     ● Brown
     ◇ Yellow

84 set collar of 5 beads

○ Green
○ Gold
■ Copper
□ Gold
○ Green

84 set collar of 5 beads

○ Green
○ Gold
■ Copper
□ Gold
○ Green

71

EVENING BAG

Really "dazzle" your friends by wearing this spectacular bag on your arm for that special evening outing.   Large enough to hold all your essentials, this bag will undoubtedly arouse interest, if not jealousy, in all who see it!

This easy-to-follow charted design will keep you busy for a while but the investment in time and beads will bring its own reward in the admiring glances for your bag.

Materials

4 vials 9 mm black bugle beads
3 vials seed beads in white
1 vial seed beads in gold
4 vials seed beads in black

Oval beads: 20 white
            20 gold

2 reels Nymo D beading thread in black

To make up the bag:

Pelmet vilene 6" x 12¼"
Black satin: 8" x 14¼", 7" x 13¼" & 5½" x 11"
Narrow elastic 9" long
Black sewing cotton

Equipment

2 beading needles
Usual sewing equipment
Sharp pointed embroidery scissors
Tray to hold beads, lined with felt

BEADING

Work the collar of the bag using white seed beads
and black bugle beads as shown on the chart (see
page 75) until you have 150 sets of beads.   Join
into a circle by passing the thread through the first
set of three beads.

Work a row of black seed beads above and below
the collar - as shown for the first amulet purse on
page 11.

Work rows 1 - 24 from the chart on page 75.

Then work all round as for the top collar, adding
sets of 1 white seed bead, 1 black bugle bead and
1 white seed bead. Add a final row of black seed
beads all round the bottom of the bag.

Fold the beaded bag in half, centralising the
pattern.

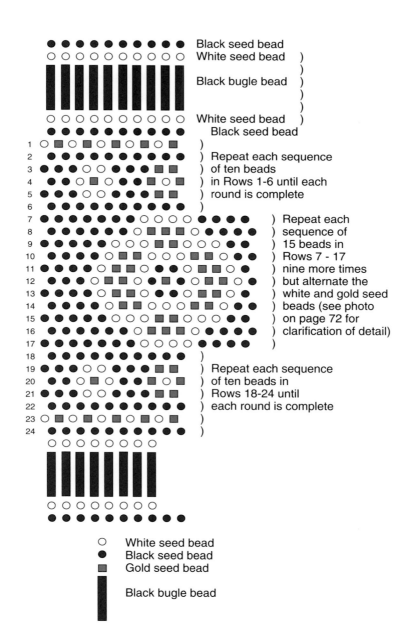

Black seed bead
White seed bead)
)
Black bugle bead)
)
)
White seed bead)
Black seed bead

1 Repeat each sequence
2 of ten beads
3 in Rows 1-6 until each
4 round is complete
5
6

7) Repeat each
8) sequence of
9) 15 beads in
10) Rows 7 - 17
11) nine more times
12) but alternate the
13) white and gold seed
14) beads (see photo
15) on page 72 for
16) clarification of detail)
17)

18)
19) Repeat each sequence
20) of ten beads in
21) Rows 18-24 until
22) each round is complete
23)
24)

○ White seed bead
● Black seed bead
▪ Gold seed bead

▮ Black bugle bead

75

FRINGE

The fringe is only added to the front of the evening bag over 75 beads. Starting at one side of the bottom edge and working from the fringe chart on page 77, repeat the sequence of 15 beads four times more to add a strand of the fringe to each of the 75 beads along the bottom edge.

HANDLE:

The handle is worked as for the top of the bag, using 120 sets of beads for the collar, and then the first six rows from the chart, repeating the sequence as before, and then repeat row 1 again.

Now work the collar rows again, using 1 white seed bead, 1 black bugle bead and 1 white seed bead, and then finally add one row of black seed beads.

Cut a strip of black satin fabric approximately 1½" wider and longer than the beaded handle. Fold over ¾" all round and lay the beaded handle over the fabric and carefully stitch the two together.

TO MAKE UP THE BAG:

Cut a piece of black satin 8" x 14¼" for the outer fabric and a piece of Pelmet Vilene 6" x 12¼" and lay this centrally over the black satin. Turn the edges of the satin over onto the Vilene and herringbone into place.

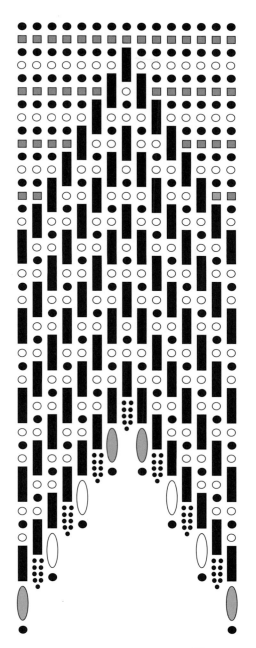

● Black seed bead
○ White seed bead
▨ Gold seed bead

▮ Black
   bugle
   bead

⬭ Gold
   oval
   bead

⬯ White
   oval
   bead

⣿ Nine
   seed
   bead
   group

Cut a piece of black satin 5½" x 11" for the inside pocket and finger fold ¼" over to the wrong side of the long edge, then fold over again to make a 1" hem. Machine stitch along the hem and again 3/8" above to form a channel. Thread the elastic through the channel and secure the ends, cutting it to be exactly the width of the lining fabric. Run a gathering thread through the lower edge about ½" in.

Cut a piece of black satin 7" x 13¼" for the lining and, with pins, mark the shorter centre line. Lay the right side of the pocket to the right side of the lining fabric, with the gathering thread laying over the line of pins. Attach the pocket to the lining by stitching through the gathering line. Fold the pocket on the line and stitch up both sides.

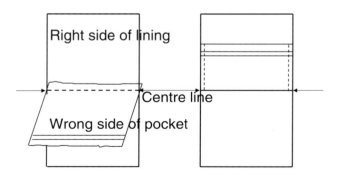

Lay the lining over the Pelmet Vilene and, folding in the edges, stitch to the prepared bag cover along each side, close to the edge. Fold in about ½" along the bottom and top edges - this can be decorated with black seed beads if desired.

Fold the bag in half and ladder stitch along each side.

Attach the beaded section over the bag, matching the top edges. The fringe will just cover the front of the bag. The top band on the back of the bag should also be stitched along its lower edge.

Attach the handle centrally, taking it inside the bag and decorating this edge with black seed beads if desired.

EVENING BAG - ENVELOPE STYLE

An alternative "clutch" bag in elegant black, with a stunning flap made from black, white and gold beads in a three-dimensional formation and a striking lining for the ultimate sensational evening outing.

Materials

For the beading:
1 vial 9mm black bugle beads
1 vial 6 mm white bugle beads
1 vial each of seed beads: White
                                       Gold
                                       Black

1 reel Nymo 'D' beading thread in black

To make up the bag:
Pelmet vilene	15" x 7"
Black satin fabric:	17" x 12"
Silky lining fabric	17" x 12"
Black press stud	
Black sewing cotton	

Equipment
Usual sewing equipment
Sharp pointed embroidery scissors
Tray to hold beads, lined with felt

BEADING

Work the central band of the bead decoration as for a "collar", following the method described in the first amulet purse, using the beads shown in the diagram below.

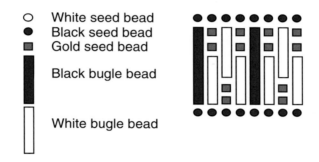

○   White seed bead
●   Black seed bead
■   Gold seed bead

     Black bugle bead

     White bugle bead

Repeat the collar sequence shown above 19 times (giving 20 sets in all), finishing with a black bugle.

Now work a series of 10 triangles below the band in the following formation: the row of black beads shown is the bottom row of the band above.

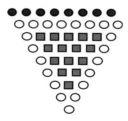

Work a second series of 10 triangles on the upper side of the band.

Then, follow the chart shown below, repeating the design five times and working into the row of black seed beads; this will give you a second layer of beads and a three-dimensional effect.

Work this row into the back of the black row of the collar:

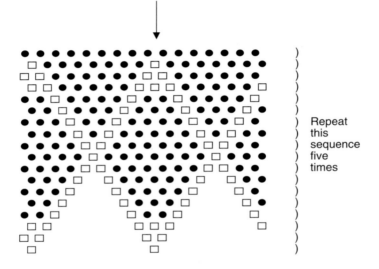

)
)
)
)
)
)
) Repeat
) this
) sequence
) five
) times
)
)
)
)
)
)

TO MAKE UP THE BAG:

Lay the pelmet Vilene over the black satin fabric and fold the edges over to the wrong side and catch down.

Cut out the silky lining fabric 1/2" larger all round and lay over the top, turning in the edges and stitch 1/8" away from the edge. At the flap end, attach the fabric with white beads.

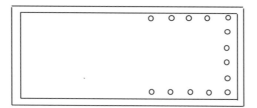

For the gusset, from the pelmet Vilene, cut two pieces in the following pattern shape, measuring 12.5 cm x 2.5cm) :

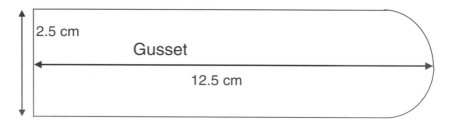

Cover with black satin, as described above, and line with the silky fabric.

Fold the main piece into the bag shape and insert the gusset, ladder-stitching into position. Centralise the beading on the flap and stitch into place. Finish with a black press stud to fasten the flap to the front of the bag.

84

GALLERY

The photographs on pages 84, 86 and 87, of an evening bag emulating The Rows in Chester, beaded containers and the decoration made by Daphne for HM The Queen's Christmas tree at Buckingham Palace are included to inspire you to Carry on Beading!

"The Rows in Chester" evening bag in the facing photograph was made as part of the Tilstone Fearnall WI's entry in a competition run by the Cheshire Federation of Women's Institutes as part of the Cheshire Agricultural Society's annual show in 1998.

On page 86, the red leather box has been decorated with beads, designed to fit exactly over the lid. The wooden box has a pattern of beads and the purse with the lipped-lid has been worked over an oval film container.

The spectacular Christmas tree decoration, which contains more than 5,000 beads, was one of a number of specially-designed hangings for the Buckingham Palace Christmas tree, which were later auctioned in aid of charity, and is included by kind permission of Fabric Flair Ltd.

Enjoy your beading and do try out some ideas of your own.

Daphne & Jackie

87